HENRY FUSELI

Frontispiece: *Self-portrait* c. 1780 chalk heightened with white 27 x 20 cm. (Victoria and Albert Museum, London)

HENRY FUSELI

Carolyn Keay

academy editions · london

st martin's press · new york

First published in Great Britain in 1974 by
Academy Editions, 7 Holland Street, London W8

SBN cloth 85670 118 1
SBN paper 85670 123 8

First published in the U.S.A. in 1974 by St. Martin's Press Inc.
175 Fifth Avenue, New York, N.Y.10010

Library of Congress Catalog Card Number 74-78462

Printed and bound in Great Britain by Burgess and Son (Abingdon) Ltd

HENRY FUSELI

The art of Henry Fuseli has never been as appreciated as it deserves. Although he was hailed in his own time as 'distinguished as a Literary Character and known to all Europe', he has too often been overlooked in the shadow of Blake or dismissed as a literary painter and illustrator. Yet he stands today as a key figure in English, if not European, art: Janus-like, one of his faces looks back to the Age of Enlightenment, the other forward to the Age of Romanticism. Sympathetic on the one hand to the discipline of Mengs and Winckelmann, yet temperamentally akin to Rousseau's outpourings of the soul, he syncretized both influences into a style which exploits the simplicity of neo-classicism with all the passion of the Romantic generation.

'Realism teams with disappointment for him whose sources of enjoyment spring in the elysium of fancy,' Fuseli declared in one of his Aphorisms. His own work is a repertoire of his fantasies, bizarre, grotesque, sublime and beautiful by turns. Although he was fiercely intellectual, the ideas distilled into his art are the emotional experiences which haunted him, the feelings of physical passion, dreams, fear, human frailty, nameless desires. For Fuseli, man's destiny is almost always damnation: the external forces exerting pressure on him are too strong. Like all visionary artists, including Blake, his moments of insight came to him rather rarely, but were so compelling that they reappear as obsessive symbols throughout his oeuvre. Some, as in his most famous picture *The Nightmare*, he reworked many times with minor variations. Others, like the flying figures of fairies and spirits, reappear in different guises in many works, from *The Shepherd's Dream* to *The Dream of Queen Katherine*. Most of all, 'dreams, and what may be called the personification of sentiment', which Fuseli considered one of the most unexplained regions of art, held an obsessive fascination for him, and the Romantic horror of these visions dominates his entire work. His illustrations to the literature of Shakespeare, Milton, Dante and the Nordic legends teem with apparitions, dreams and the supernatural, varying in form and intensity from the demoniacal and cosmic figures of the Milton cycle, through the ethereal calligraphic lines of *Aphrodite carrying off Paris* to the comforting solidity of the Ghost in Hamlet. *The Nightmare* is almost the dream of a nightmare. In *Chriemhild in a dream sees Siegfried dead* we experience the supra-reality of foreseeing the death of the hero while he stands by looking on.

Obsessive images of reclining female forms, lascivious love and harlots also recur, from the overt sexual debauchery of *Three nude women and an amorino surround a prostrate man* to the heavy symbolism of *The Nightmare*. This painting, in its many forms, is a sublimation of the artist's erotic passion for Anna Landolt of Zurich, a work of supernatural retribution to punish her for not requiting his love. The back of the painting bears her portrait. A sexual symbolism also underlies many apparently innocuous drawings, such as the motif of a girl at a spinet, which was a seventeenth-century invention representing the transition between virginity and the breaking of the hymeneal chord. Yet this erotic cynicism and fantasy which is unleashed in both his writings and drawings is firmly restrained both in the many prim portraits of his wife, whom he married at the age of forty seven, and in his recognition of the good and faithful wife in *Ulysses and Penelope* and *The Return of Milton's Wife*.

Fuseli's love of allegorical allusion and symbolism, sexual, moral, satirical, even political, rides unfettered throughout all his work. Tomory (*The Life and Art of Henry Fuseli*, London 1972) sees *Thor battering the Midgard Serpent* as 'a contemporary allegory of events in France, for Thor, crass, bestial but courageous was the hero of the Norse lower classes . . . so democratic Virtue overcomes the strangling coils of hereditary Vice.' A more bitter and personal comment lies behind the satirical sketch Fuseli sent to Northcote on his departure from Rome, which shows the artist defecating on Switzerland, his birthplace (where he broke his journey for a short while) while the phallus-bird of his soul soars away from the competition of the mice in England back towards Italy.

5

Fuseli's own particular vision and ideas find their purest expression in the tonal and linear unity of his graphic art, which allowed him a grace and movement less natural in oil. He concentrated and distilled his images into pictorial essences and symbols, in some cases almost to abstraction, as in the drawing of *Fear: three crouching girls*. It is his calligraphic line which fixes the moment of terror and drama, captures the charged atmosphere and betrays character and emotion in his work. Colour is reduced to a minimal range of tonal contrasts. This virtual negation effects a suspension of the consciousness of time and limits the spatial context in the drawings to a no-man's-land of sober gravity. Yet within this simplification his technical proficiency with washtones can produce the smoothness of skin, the hardness of marble, and the coldness of ice. The heavy dead colour of his oil paintings creates the same atmosphere of timelessness and mystery which releases his figures from the bonds of reality into a different fantastic world.

> Every artist has, or ought to have, a character or system of his own: if, instead of referring to the test of nature, you judge him by your own packed notions, or arraign him at the tribunal of schools which he does not recognise – you degrade the dignity of art, and add another fool to the herd of the Dilettanti.　　　　　　　　　　　　　　　　　　　Corollary to Aphorism 18

Self-taught, and owing allegiance to no particular school, Fuseli belonged to a generation which no longer subscribed to the 'grand manner' of Joshua Reynolds, nor any unifying style. It was Reynolds himself, later President of the Royal Academy, who finally encouraged him to abandon his literary projects and devote himself seriously to an artistic career. His eight years in Rome, studying and executing commissions for visitors, brought him into contact with the great masters and many contemporary artists, and he followed what he called the 'modern eclectic principle', drawing on models as varied as Piranesi, Michelangelo, Rubens, Alexander Runciman and J. H. Mortimer. Rosa he admired as having a 'lively and vigorous imagination'; Hogarth's engravings he considered 'exquisite'. His Zurich sketchbook contains many single heads from Raphael's frescoes. The theatre, also, was a major influence in his work. Fuseli was an avid theatre-goer all his life, which covered a particularly brilliant episode in the history of the London stage. Stylistically, it is present in the exaggerated gesture of the traditional declamatory style of acting, and in the reduction to a minimum of stage properties and furniture included in his paintings. Moreover the angle of view of most of his works, with the figures high against a low horizon, gives the viewer the impression of watching from the pit. The theatre also figures largely in Fuseli's choice of subject, providing both the moment of terror and the allegorical symbolism which so appealed to him. Although he sometimes drew from life – *Garrick as the Duke of Gloucester* and *Kemble as Hotspur and Glendower* – it was the moral strength of Shakespeare he was depicting. In Fuseli's eyes, Shakespeare was 'the great instructor of mankind' who 'afflicts innocence and virtue', and was an endless source of material for his own work.

The influences on Fuseli during his earlier life were no less diverse. Born Johann Heinrich Füssli in Zurich on 6 February 1741, he grew up in an atmosphere of progressive and radical ideas which included many of the famous names of the *Sturm und Drang* period. A fellow student with him at the Zurich Collegium was Johann Kaspar Lavater, with whom Fuseli (the spelling he was eventually to adopt in England) kept up a lifelong intimate correspondence. Lavater used several of Fuseli's drawings to illustrate his famous *Essays on Physignomy*. At the Collegium, too, the teachings of the republican philosopher J. J. Bodmer fostered a permanent love for poetry and introduced him to many literary sources which were to inspire his art. Fuseli acknowledges his debt to Bodmer in a painting which depicts his mentor in a triangle of forces with Sulzer and Waser, and the artist himself as a passive observer in the wings. But Zurich was too provincial; Fuseli longed for England and its promise of liberty. After a brief but stimulating stay in Germany where he met Sulzer, J. J. Spalding and the Romantic poet Klopstock, he came to London in 1764, where he supported himself by doing hack translations. He knew Greek, Latin, Hebrew, French, Italian and English, although several anecdotes record his highly accented pronunciation of the last. Among other things he translated Winckelmann's *Reflections on the Paintings and Sculptures of the Greeks,* one of the formative works of neo-classicism. However in 1707 he definitively declared his allegiance to the Romantic camp with his anonymous pamphlet *Remarks on the Writings and Conduct of J-J. Rousseau.*

Small in stature, (he was not much taller than five feet), often aggressive, intolerant of fools and often of his intellectual peers, witty and sceptical, and a supporter of the abolition of slavery, the 'wild Swiss' was one of the most interesting creative minds in both the literary and artistic circles of London. Often attacked by the critics and misunderstood by the public — Walpole's famous comment on seeing *The Mandrake* (1785) was 'Shockingly mad, mad, mad, madder than ever.' — he was however respected and seldom ignored. His caustic lines in *The Dunciad of Painting* (1780-89) make no secret of his contempt for some members of the artistic world:

Love without Fire; Smiles without Mirth; bright Tears
To Grief unknown; and without Beauty, Airs;
Celestial Harlots; Graces dressed by France;
Rosy Despair and Passions taught to dance
Irradiate the gay leaf — then charm struck crowd
Devoutly gaze, then burst in raptures loud.

At 38 he was a late starter to a serious artistic career, but he was never short of commissions from patrons and admirers. He was a keen contributor, along with Reynolds, Northcote, West and Barry, to the Shakespeare Gallery scheme of Alderman Boydell, and worked for years on his own Milton Gallery project, supported only by subscriptions from friends and often close to penury. The exhibition itself was a failure, but the project gained him considerable esteem in the last years of his life, and although now largely lost to us, it was probably the last of the monumental cycles in European art.

Fuseli ended his career as Professor of Painting at the Royal Academy, well-known for his animated and boldly original lectures and numbering among his pupils nearly all the famous names of the succeeding generation — Etty, Landseer, Haydon, Wilkie, Mulready and Leslie. 'Poetic painting', a phrase often repeated in his lectures, neatly sums up his own work: rather than the slavish illustration of literary texts, it is the expression of Romantic and soaring fantasy. His own powerful and unique vision transcends his subjects and at its best touches the sublime, so that in the last analysis we can do no more than bow to his demands and 'referring to the text of nature', judge him by his own criteria.

Select Bibliography

Antal, Frederick   *Fuseli Studies,* London 1956

Boase, T. S. R.   *English Art 1800-1870,* Oxford 1959

Kalman, Harold D.   'Füssli, Pope and the Nightmare', *Pantheon,* III, 1971

Knowles, John   *The Life and Writings of Henry Fuseli, Esq., MARA,* 3 vols, London 1831

Schiff, Gert   *Zeichnungen von Johann Heinrich Füssli,* Zurich 1959

Schiff, Gert   *Johann Heinrich Füssli: Oeuvrekatalog,* Zurich 1973

Todd, Ruthven   *Tracks in the Snow,* London 1946

Tomory, Peter   *The Life and Art of Henry Fuseli,* London 1972

Arts Council of Great Britain   *Fuseli* Exhibition Catalogue, London 1950

Kunsthaus Zurich   *Johann Heinrich Füssli* Exhibition Catalogue, Zurich 1969

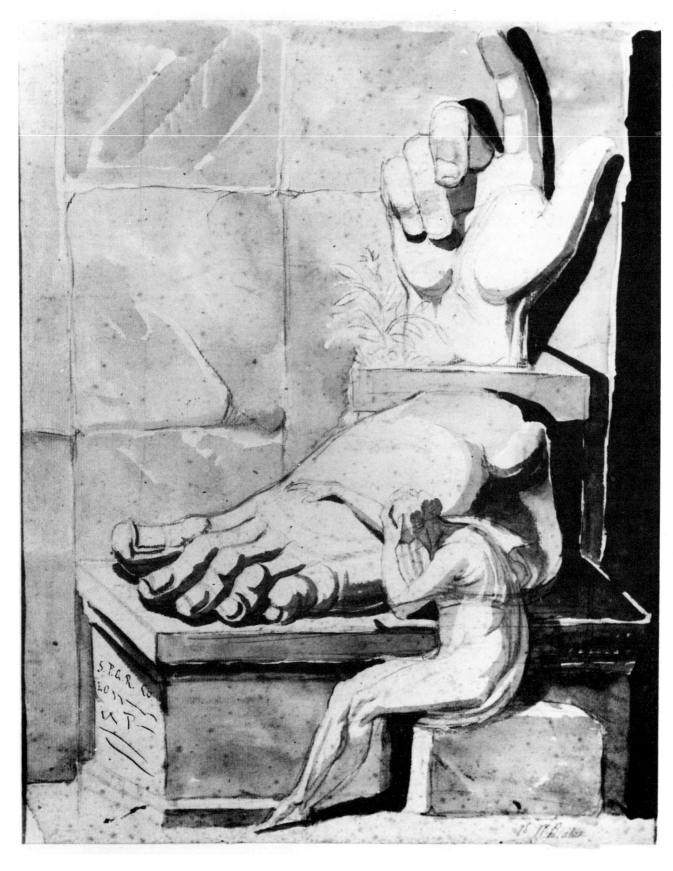

1.   *The artist in despair over the magnitude of antique fragments* c. 1778-80 red chalk and sepia wash 42 x 35.2 cm.
(Kunsthaus, Zurich)

2.   *The artist in conversation with J. J. Bodmer* 1778-81 oil on canvas 163 x 150 cm. (Kunsthaus, Zurich)

3. *Caricature satire of the artist leaving Italy* 1778 pen 24.5 x 19.3 cm. (Kunsthaus, Zurich)

4. *A capriccio of the horse tamers* c. 1810-15   pencil with blue and grey wash 46.6 x 31 cm.
(Auckland City Art Gallery)

5.   *Undine displeased leaves the fisherman's hut* 1822 pencil, blue and grey wash 32 x 37.6 cm. (Kunsthaus, Zurich)

6.   *Undine and Huldbrand* c. 1819-22 pencil and watercolour 48.1 x 31.9 cm. (Auckland City Art Gallery)

7. *Undine comes to the fisherman's hut* 1821 oil on canvas 63.5 x 76.5 cm. (Öffentliche Kunstsammlung, Basle)

8. *Siegfried and Chriemhild* 1807 watercolour 48 x 36 cm. (Auckland City Art Gallery)

15

9. *William Tell escaping from Gessler* 1787, engraved C. G. Guttenburg (Victoria and Albert Museum, London)

10. *Chriemhild in a dream sees Siegfried dead* 1805 pencil, watercolour and body colour
38.5 x 48.5 cm. (Kunsthaus, Zurich)

11. *Garrick as Duke of Gloucester (Richard III; 1, 2)* 1766 pen, pencil and wash 31.7 x 45.7 cm. (Kunsthaus, Zurich)

12. *The oath on the Rütli* 1778-81 oil on canvas 267 x 178 cm. (Rathaus, Zurich)

19

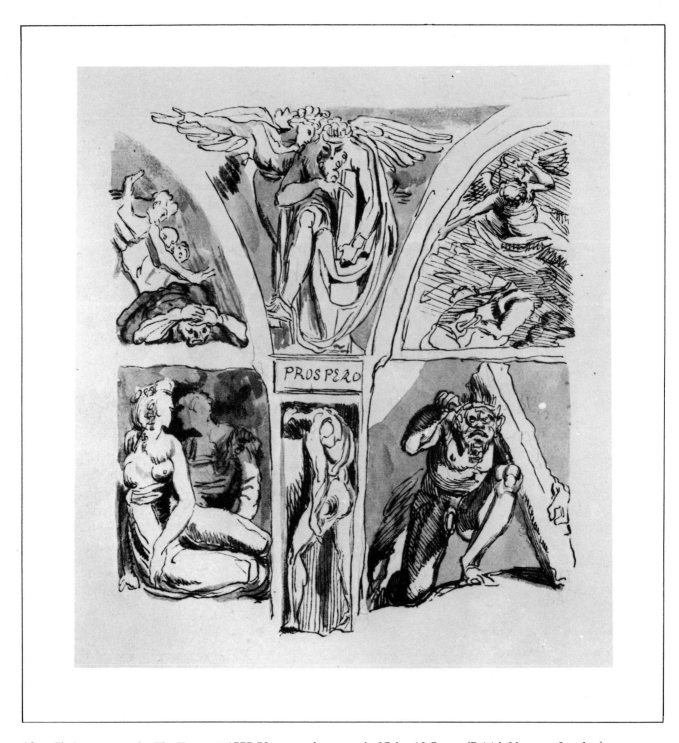

13. *Shakespeare cycle: The Tempest* 1777-78 pen and grey wash 27.2 x 19.7 cm. (British Museum, London)

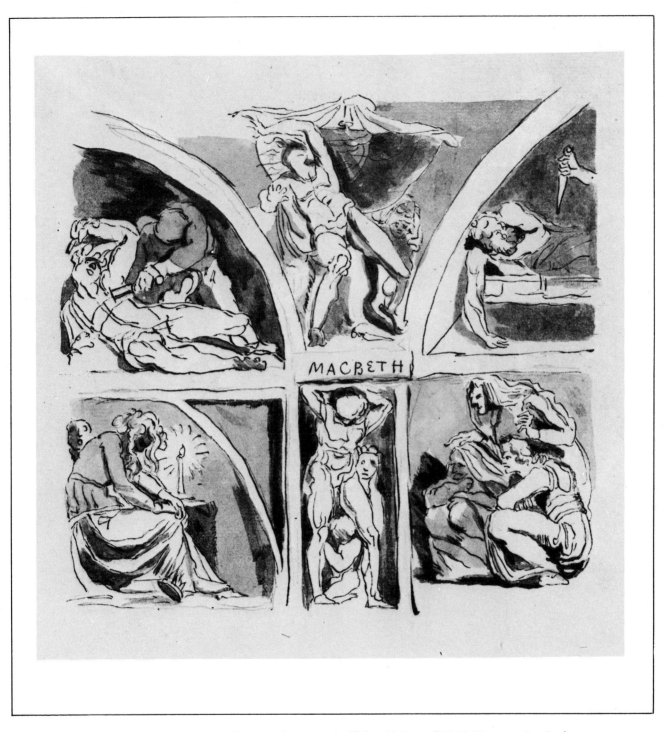

14.   *Shakespeare cycle: Macbeth* 1777-78 pen and grey wash 27.3 x 19.6 cm. (British Museum, London)

15. *A scene from Timon of Athens* 1783 pen and brown ink with brown, yellow and pink wash on oiled paper
20.5 x 29.9 cm. (Auckland City Art Gallery)

16. *Hamlet and the ghost* 1789 Boydell Shakespeare Gallery, engraved R. Thew, 1803 (Royal Academy, London)

17. *Othello* from the Rivington *Shakespeare* 1805, engraved R. Rhodes
18. *Macbeth* from the Rivington *Shakespeare* 1805, engraved C. Warren

19. *A winter's tale* from the Rivington *Shakespeare* 1805, engraved J. Neagle

20. *The comedy of errors* from the Rivington *Shakespeare* 1805, engraved I. Milton

21. *Romeo and Juliet* from the Rivington *Shakespeare* 1805, engraved W. Blake

22. *Anthony and Cleopatra* from the Rivington *Shakespeare* 1805, engraved R. H. Cromek

26

23. *Hamlet, Horatio and the gravedigger* 1802 pen with grey, blue and pink wash 37.5 x 29.5 cm. (Auckland City Art Gallery)

24. *Lady Macbeth sleepwalking* c. 1775-76 pen and grey wash 30.7 x 43.2 cm. (British Museum, London)

25. *Warwick vowing vengeance on the dead body of Gloucester* 1777 pen and wash 25.4 x 37.7 cm. (British Museum, London)

26. *Titania finds the ring on the shore* 1804-05 oil on canvas 61 x 45 cm. (Kunsthaus, Zurich)

27. *The death of Cardinal Beaufort* 1772 pen and grey wash over pencil 65 x 81 cm.
(Walker Art Gallery, Liverpool)

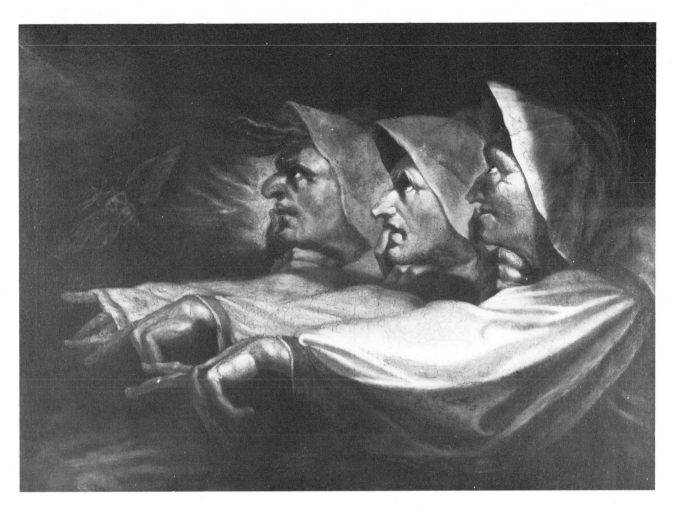

28.   *The three witches* 1783 oil on canvas 65 x 92 cm. (Kunsthaus, Zurich)

29.   *The death of Brutus* c. 1775-80 black chalk 53.5 x 66 cm. (British Museum, London)

30.   *'Here I and Sorrow sit' from Shakespeare's King John* 1783 oil on canvas 63.5 x 53.8 cm. (Smith College Museum of Art, Northampton, Mass)

31. *Julius Caesar* from the Rivington *Shakespeare* 1805, engraved C. Warren

32. *Hamlet* from the Rivington *Shakespeare* 1805, engraved Joseph Smith

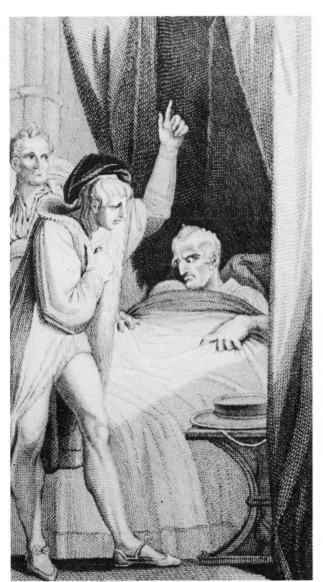 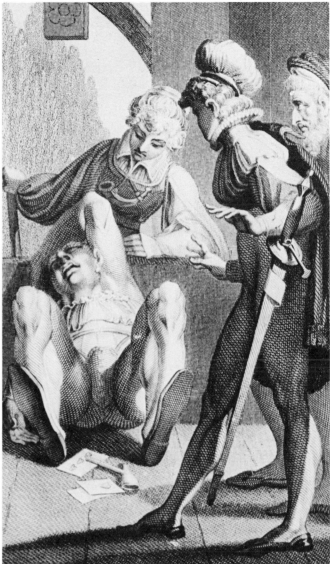

33. *The death of Cardinal Beaufort* from the Rivington *Shakespeare* 1805, engraved R. H. Cromek

34. *The taming of the Shrew* from the Rivington *Shakespeare* 1805, engraved C. Warren

35. *Lear, Cornwall, Albany, Goneril, Regan, Cordelia, King of France, Duke of Burgundy, Kent and attendants* 1789
Boydell Shakespeare Gallery, engraved R. Earlom, 1803 (Royal Academy, London)

36. *Falstaff in the buckbasket* 1792 oil on canvas 135 x 169 cm. (Kunsthaus, Zurich)

37. *Falstaff with Doll Tearsheet* 1789 Boydell Shakespeare Gallery, engraved W. Leney 1803 (Royal Academy, London)

I   *Thor battering the Midgard Serpent* 1790 oil on canvas 131 x 92 cm. (Royal Academy, London)
II (overleaf) *The shepherd's dream* 1793 oil on canvas 155 x 215 cm. (Tate Gallery, London)

38.   *Dante on the ice of Cocytus* 1774 pen and grey wash 30.5 x 38.5 cm. (British Museum, London)

III   *The dispute between Hotspur, Glendower, Mortimer and Worcester about the division of England* 1784 oil on canvas 210 x 180 cm. (Birmingham Museum and Art Gallery)

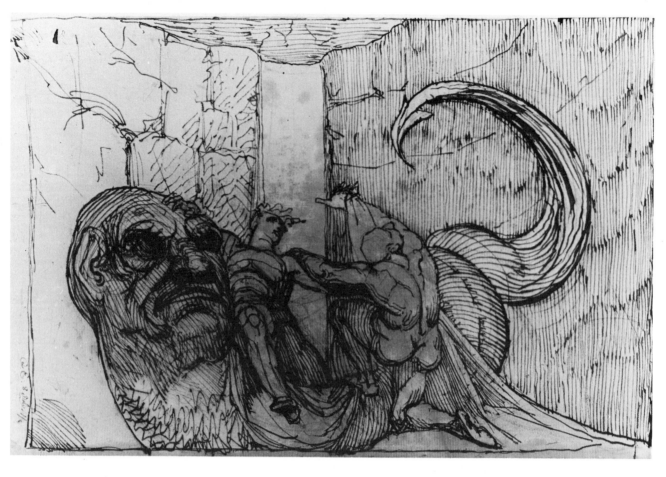

41. *Dante and Vergil before Cavalcanti and Farinata* 1774 pen and watercolour 25.9 x 27.1 cm. (British Museum, London)

39. *Vergil, Dante and Geryon* 1811 pen and brown ink 19.8 x 29.3 cm. (Auckland City Art Gallery)

40. *Vergil, Dante and Geryon* (verso, drawn through from recto) 1811 pen with yellow and pink 19.8 x 29.3 cm. (Auckland City Art Gallery)

43. *Subject from Milton's L'Allegro* c. 1780 pencil heightened with white 33 x 41.1 cm. (Auckland City Art Gallery)

42. *The serpent tempting Eve* 1802 oil on panel 30.2 x 23.8 cm. (Auckland City Art Gallery)

45. *Britomart frees Amoret from Busirane* 1793 pen and crayon 36.1 x 49 cm. (Kunsthaus, Zurich)

44. *Death and Sin bridging the 'Waste' of Chaos and met by Satan on his return from Earth* c. 1819-21 pencil, pen and watercolour 39.3 x 31.5 cm. (Auckland City Art Gallery)

46. *Ezzelin Bracciaferro musing over the dead Meduna* 1779 red chalk, pen and wash 34.5 x 40.5 cm. (British Museum, London)

IV *Titania and Bottom* 1786-89 oil on canvas 216 x 274 cm. (Tate Gallery, London)

V *Percival delivering Belisane from the spell of Urma* 1783 oil on canvas 99 x 125 cm. (Tate Gallery, London)

VI *The nightmare* 1790-91 oil on canvas 76 x 63 cm. (Goethe Museum, Frankfurt)

47.   *The appearance of Christ at Emmaus* 1792 oil on canvas 143.5 x 118.1 cm. (Collection of Mr and Mrs Paul Mellon)

48.   *The dream of Belinda* 1799 oil on canvas 103 x 123 cm. (Vancouver Art Gallery)

49.   *Achilles grasps at the soul of Patroclus* 1803 oil on canvas 91 x 71 cm. (Kunsthaus, Zurich)

50.   *Study* n.d. pen and wash 38 x 25.6 cm. (British Museum, London)

51.   *Fortuna hovering above the world* 1780-90 pen 23.5 x 19 cm. (British Museum, London)

52.   *Ajax raging* c. 1770-72 pen and red crayon 28 x 33 cm. (Kunsthaus, Zurich)

53. *The witch and the mandrake* c. 1812-13 soft ground etching 45.7 x 55.7 cm. (The Metropolitan Museum of Art, New York; Elisha Whittelsey Fund 1953)

54. *The conversion of St. Paul* 1770 pen and wash 17.3 x 27.7 cm. (British Museum, London)

55. *Hephaestus, Bia and Crato securing Prometheus on Mount Caucasus* c. 1810
pen, pencil, grey and pink wash 35.9 x 30.2 cm. (Auckland City Art Gallery)

56.   *The vision of the lazar house* 1791-93 pencil heightened with white fixative 56.5 x 66 cm. (Kunsthaus, Zurich)

57. *Composition of Raphael, drawn from memory* from Lavater *Essays on Physiognomy* 1792, engraved T. Holloway

58. *Isis, from Plutarch's Isis and Osiris* 1805-10 pencil and
wash 40 x 32 cm. (British Museum, London)

61. *Eros and Psyche* 1808 pencil, pen and watercolour 23.3 x 35.8 cm. (Auckland City Art Gallery)

59. *Caius Marius and the Cimbrian soldier* c. 1764-65 pen and grey wash 30.6 x 48.6 cm. (Auckland City Art Gallery)

60. *The witch of Endor* 1777 from Lavater *Essays on Physiognomy* 1792, engraved T. Holloway

62. *The escapee* 1772 pen and wash 38 x 64 cm. (British Museum, London)

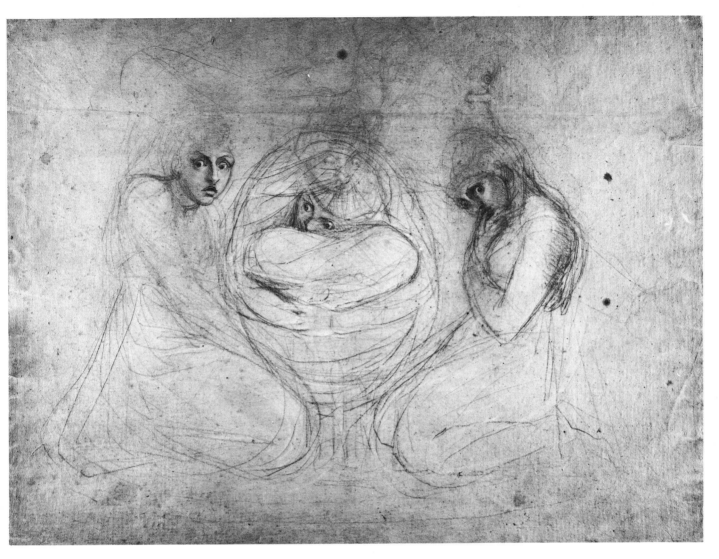

63. *Fear: three crouching girls* c. 1780-82 pencil and white chalk 40.1 x 53.7 cm. (Kunsthaus, Zurich)

64. *Three female nudes and an amorino surround a prostrate male figure* (verso) 1811 pencil
20 x 27.1 cm. (Auckland City Art Gallery)

VII *The death of Oedipus* 1784 oil on canvas 150 x 166 cm. (Walker Art Gallery, Liverpool)

72

65. *Parental care* c. 1805 pen with grey and blue wash 19.2 x 28.8 cm. (Auckland City Art Gallery)

VIII *Garrick and Mrs Pritchard as Macbeth and Lady Macbeth* 1812 oil on canvas 101 x 127 cm. (Tate Gallery, London)

IX *The return of Milton's wife* 1796-99 oil on canvas 88 x 111 cm. (Walker Art Gallery, Liverpool)

66. *Portrait of Mrs. Fuseli* 1794 pencil and watercolour heightened with white
34.6 x 21.6 cm. (Ulster Museum, Belfast)

67. *Folly and innocence* 1800 pencil and brown wash 42.4 x 25.6 cm.
(Museum and Art Gallery, Nottingham)

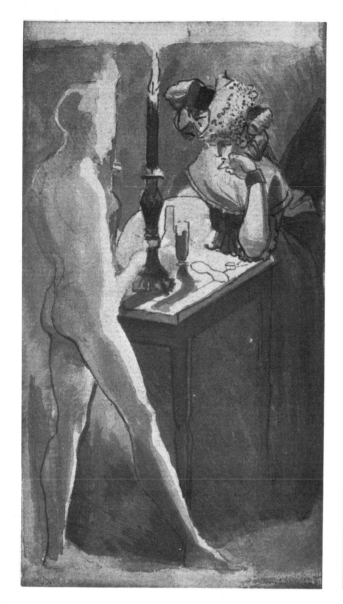

68. *Naked ithyphallic man or ghost with a woman at a table* c. 1814 brush drawing with brown and pink wash 16.7 x 9.2 cm. (Private collection)

69. *Woman at a dressing table* 1810-20 pen and brown ink over black chalk 16.3 x 9.4 cm. (Private collection)

70. *Two lesbians looking in a mirror* 1810-20 pen and brown ink over black chalk 17.4 x 12.5 cm. (Private collection)

74. *Allegory of vanity* 1811 pencil, pen and watercolour 20 x 27.1 cm. (Auckland City Art Gallery)

71. *Mrs Fuseli sleeping* c. 1795 pen and brown ink, with grey, blue and pink wash 22.7 x 18.6 cm.
(Auckland City Art Gallery)

72. *Woman gazing in a mirror* c. 1814 pen and watercolour 16 x 9 cm. (Ashmolean Museum, Oxford)

73. *A woman in tudor costume* c. 1803 pen 22 x 16.5 cm. (Royal Academy, London)

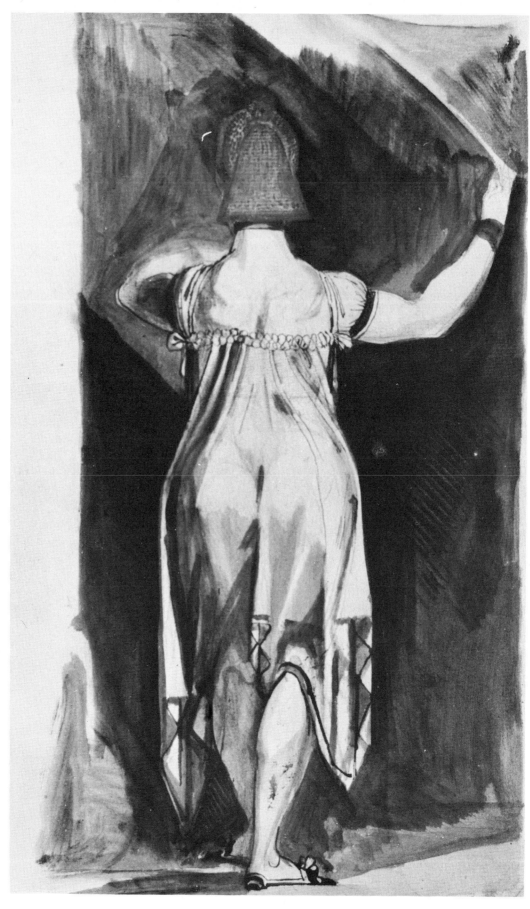

75. *A woman standing, seen from the back, drawing a curtain aside* c. 1790-1800 pen, pencil,
with grey, brown and pink wash 30.7 x 17.3 cm. (Auckland City Art Gallery)

76.   *A young man kissing a girl at a spinet* 1819 black crayon 24.7 x 20 cm. (Kunsthaus, Zurich)

81

77. *Study of nude man* pen   32.4 x 19.7 cm. (Royal Academy, London)

78. *Nude man* (verso) pen 32.4 x 19.7 cm. (Royal Academy, London)

79. *Bust portrait of Mrs Fuseli* c. 1790-95 pen with black and blue wash, heightened with white 17.4 x 14.4 cm.
(Auckland City Art Gallery)

81. *Girl on a sofa looking out of a window* 1803 polyautograph 21.6 x 31.7 cm. (Victoria and Albert Museum, London)

80. *Woman with a stiletto* c. 1816-17 pencil and black chalk 20.1 x 14.5 cm. (Ashmolean Museum, Oxford)

82. *A woman before the Laocoön* c. 1802 pen 32 x 41 cm. (Kunsthaus, Zurich)

83. *The debutante*   1807 pen and red wash 37 x 24 cm. (Tate Gallery, London)

84. *Mrs Fuseli seated at a table* c. 1790-92 pen with grey, brown and pink wash 22.7 x 15.7 cm. (Auckland City Art Gallery)

78-04840